**NPLF**
Nashville Public Library FOUNDATION

*This book given
to the Nashville Public Library
through the generosity of the*
**Dollar General
Literacy Foundation**

NPLF.ORG

# Games
## AROUND the WORLD

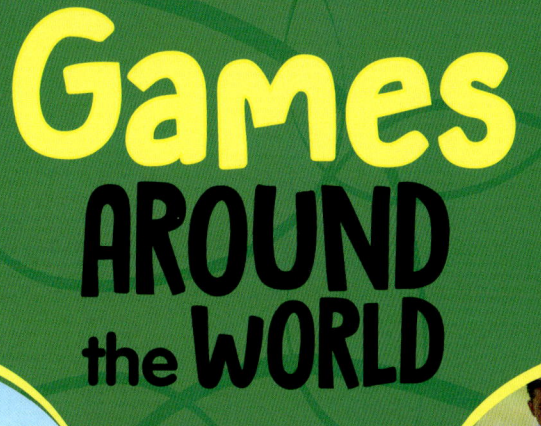

by John Perritano

Children's Press®
An imprint of Scholastic Inc.

Library of Congress Cataloging-in-Publication Data
Names: Perritano, John, author.
Title: Games around the world/John Perritano.
Description: First edition. | New York: Children's Press an imprint of Scholastic Inc., 2021. |
  Series: Around the world | Includes index. | Audience: Ages 5–7. | Audience: Grades K–1. |
  Summary: "This book introduces young readers to some of the many ways people play games around the world"— Provided by publisher.
Identifiers: LCCN 2021000148 (print) | LCCN 2021000149 (ebook) | ISBN 9781338768701 (library binding) |
  ISBN 9781338768718 (paperback) | ISBN 9781338768725 (ebook)
Subjects: LCSH: Games—Juvenile literature. | Games—Cross-cultural studies—Juvenile literature.
Classification: LCC HQ782 .P397 2021 (print) | LCC HQ782 (ebook) | DDC 796.1/4—dc23
LC record available at https://lccn.loc.gov/2021000148
LC ebook record available at https://lccn.loc.gov/2021000149

Copyright © 2022 by Scholastic Inc.

All rights reserved. Published by Children's Press, an imprint of Scholastic Inc., *Publishers since 1920*. SCHOLASTIC, CHILDREN'S PRESS, AROUND THE WORLD™, and associated logos are trademarks and/or registered trademarks of Scholastic Inc.

The publisher does not have any control over and does not assume any responsibility for author or third-party websites or their content.

No part of this publication may be reproduced, stored in a retrieval system, or transmitted in any form or by any means, electronic, mechanical, photocopying, recording, or otherwise, without written permission of the publisher. For information regarding permission, write to Scholastic Inc., Attention: Permissions Department, 557 Broadway, New York, NY 10012.

10 9 8 7 6 5 4 3 2 1     22 23 24 25 26

Printed in Heshan, China 62
First edition, 2022

Series produced by Spooky Cheetah Press
Cover and book design by Kimberly Shake

Photos ©: cover top left, 1 top left: Free2barredo/Wikimedia; cover top right, 1 top right: ZUMA Press Inc/Alamy Images; cover bottom left, 1 bottom left: Trevor Thompson/Alamy Images; 4 left: Erika Santelices/AFP/Getty Images; 4 center: Alexander Zemlianichenko/AP Images; 4 right: Hedayatullah Amid/EPA-EFE/Shutterstock; 5 left: Stephen Dorey/Alamy Images; 6: Julie Campbell/Dreamstime; 7: Michele Burgess/Alamy Images; 8: Free2barredo/Wikimedia; 9: WBC ART/Alamy Images; 10: Mike Clarke/AFP/Getty Images; 11: ViewStock/agefotostock; 12: Callie Lipkin/Gallery Stock; 13: ZUMA Press Inc/Alamy Images; 14: Grabka/laif/Redux; 15: Mohammad Ismail/Reuters/Alamy Images; 17: vgajic/Getty Images; 18: davidf/Getty Images; 19: Tatyana Tomsickova/Dreamstime; 21: Popperfoto/Getty Images; 22: Pontus Edenberg/Dreamstime; 23: Selamed Riyanto/EyeEm/Getty Images; 24: Philimon Bulawayo/Reuters/Alamy Images; 25: RedChopsticks/Getty Images; 26–27 background: Jim McMahon/Mapman ®; 26 bottom: Tina Manley/Alamy Images; 27 top left: Dan Kenyon/Getty Images; 27 top right: Trevor Thompson/Alamy Images; 28 left: Mariela Lombard/ZUMA Press/Alamy Images; 28 center: Roz Bannan/Getty Images; 28 right: George Sweeney/Alamy Images; 29 top: Daniel Smith/Getty Images; 29 bottom left: Yuri Cortez/AFP/Getty Images; 29 bottom center: Peter Charlesworth/LightRocket/Getty Images.

All other photos © Shutterstock.

# TABLE of CONTENTS

**INTRODUCTION**
Just Like Me  **4**

**CHAPTER 1**
You Are It  **6**

**CHAPTER 2**
Gotcha!  **12**

**CHAPTER 3**
Having a Ball  **19**

**CHAPTER 4**
All the Marbles  **22**

If You Lived Here …  **26**

A Closer Look  **28**

Glossary  **30**

Index/About the Author  **32**

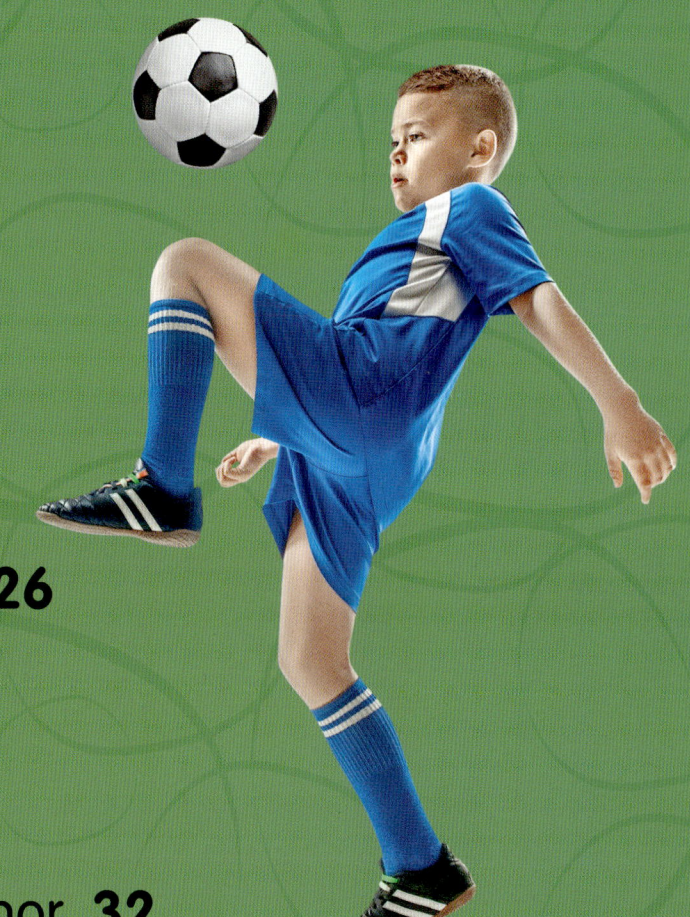

introduction

# JUST LIKE ME

Kids in every country around the world have a lot in common. They go to school and play. They have families and friends. Still, some things—like games they play—can be very different!

DOMINICAN REPUBLIC

GREECE

AFGHANISTAN

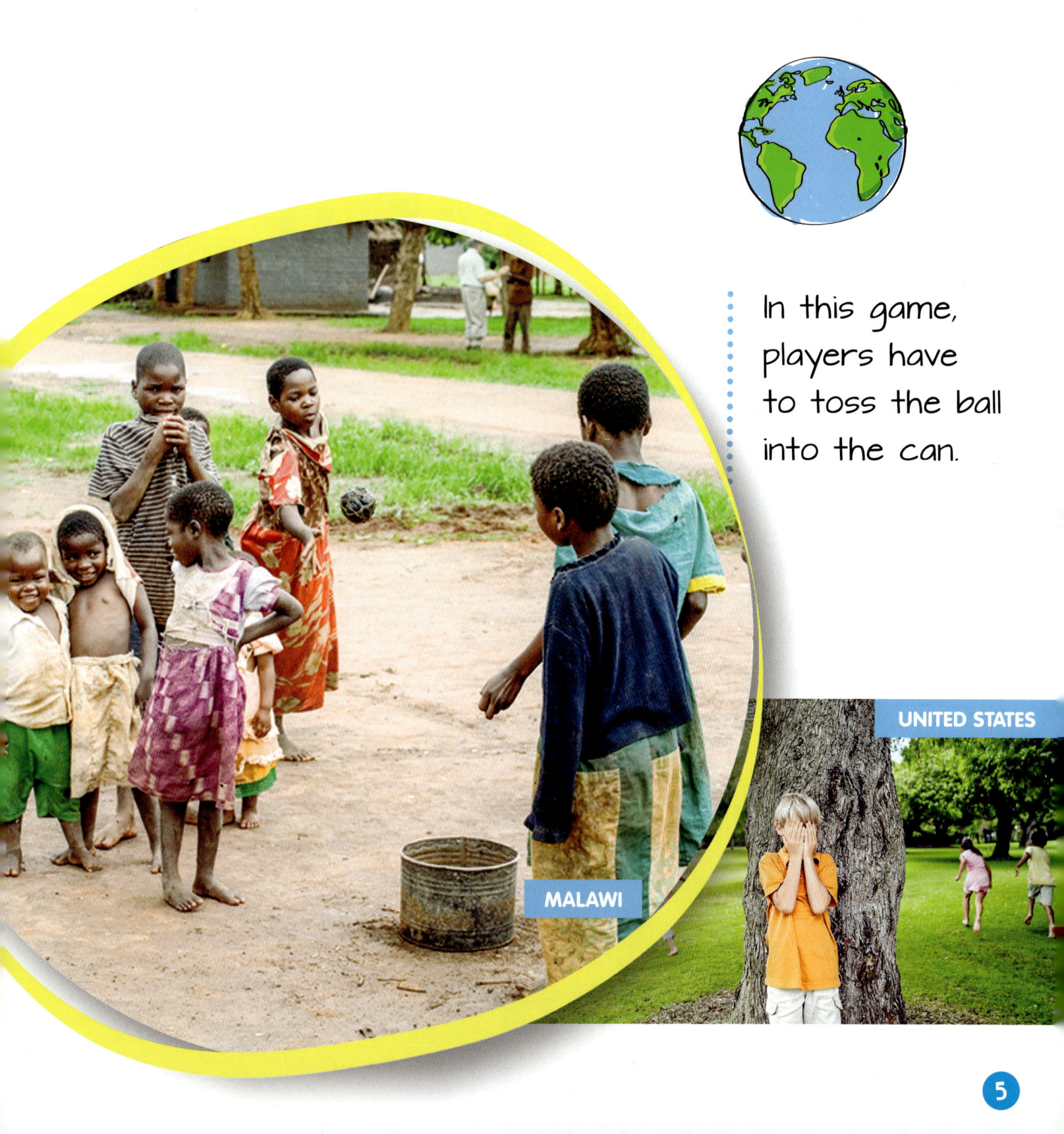

In this game, players have to toss the ball into the can.

MALAWI

UNITED STATES

## chapter 1
# YOU ARE IT

There are many ways to play tag. In Turkey, kids play run away rabbit. Players form a circle around one child—the rabbit. Another player, the hound, is outside the circle. The kids in the circle say a **rhyme**. When the rhyme ends, the rabbit runs out of the circle and is chased by the hound.

In the United States, kids play duck, duck, goose, which is similar to run away rabbit.

When kids in Turkey play this game, the rabbit becomes the hound after being caught.

Filipino is spoken in the Philippines. In that language, *baka* means "cow."

8

Children in the Philippines play a game called luksong baka (LUCK-san BAW-kah). It is like a combination of tag and leapfrog. But there are two big differences. In luksong baka, players don't hop over a frog. They jump over a cow. Any jumper who touches the cow becomes the next baka.

Children have been playing some form of leapfrog for hundreds of years.

In China, kids play a game called catch the dragon's tail. The players form a line and hold on to the person in front of them. The person at the front, or head, of the dragon must try to tag the person at the end of the line. The rest of the kids twist and turn to keep the tail safe.

Dragons play an important role in Chinese **culture**.

In catch the dragon's tail, if any player lets go, he or she is out.

## chapter 2
# GOTCHA!

In some games, the goal is to take something from another player. In the United States, some kids play flag football. Teams score points by carrying the ball over the goal line for a touchdown. Players on the other team try to snatch a flag hanging from the ball carrier's waist to stop him or her from scoring.

In capture the flag, there are two teams. Each tries to steal the other's flag.

A team can throw a pass for a touchdown or run the ball into the end zone.

13

In Afghanistan, the kite fight is called *jang*.

In Afghanistan, children play a game called kite fighting. Players fly their kites into each other's, hitting the strings together. The goal is to cut the string of the other player's kite. The winner is the person whose string is uncut and whose kite is still flying.

In Afghanistan, kite flying is considered an art.

In France, children play a game called exchange. Players sit in a circle of chairs, each with a different number. One player, who is blindfolded, stands in the circle and calls out two numbers. The players in those numbered seats must switch chairs before the blindfolded player can sit on one.

Exchange is similar to musical chairs, which is played in the United States.

This French game is most fun when played with 10 or more players!

Australia's mild weather makes it a great place for outdoor games.

chapter 3
# HAVING A BALL

There are hundreds of games that can be played with a ball. In Australia, kids play kai (KIGH). Players stand in a circle, and then someone throws a ball into the air. Players pass the ball to one another by smacking it with their hands. The player who lets the ball hit the ground is out.

Kai can also be played with a balloon.

Soccer is one of the most popular games in the world. Outside the United States, it is called football. In Bolivia, many children play soccer in the streets. Rules can vary, but players still have to kick a ball into a goal. Some of the world's best soccer players grew up playing street soccer.

Kids often play with **homemade** soccer balls.

In Bolivia, a game of street soccer can break out at any time!

## chapter 4
# ALL THE MARBLES

In Indonesia, kids play kelereng (ca-LAIR-eng). To play the game, kids put their marbles in a group. Each player keeps one striker marble. The players take turns shooting their striker at the group of marbles. The shooter keeps any marbles he or she hits.

Kids can play marbles alone or with others.

Kelereng is also called *gundu* in Indonesia.

In Zimbabwe, kids often use stones in place of marbles.

Kudoda (koo-DO-dah) is a game from Zimbabwe that can be played with marbles or stones. Stones are placed inside a circle. A player tosses one stone in the air and picks up as many others as possible before the tossed stone hits the ground.

One thing all these games have in common is that they are fun to play! What types of games do you like to play?

Kids can use marbles to play many different games, including Chinese checkers.

# IF YOU LIVED HERE...

Let's look at some other fun games around the world!

**GUATEMALA**
Trompos is a game of battling tops. The goal is for one player to knock over another's top.

**UNITED STATES**
When playing hide-and-seek, the seeker tries to find and tag other players before they reach home base.

### IRELAND
Shadows is a game where one player captures another by standing on his or her shadow.

### INDIA
Teams take turns chasing and defending when playing kho kho (KOH koh), the oldest tagging game in India.

### NIGERIA
Kids play a clapping, skip-jumping game that is a little like follow the leader. One player tries to guess the other player's next leg movements and mirror them.

# A CLOSER LOOK

Football takes on many forms and names depending on where people live.

## United States

Here, the game is played with an oblong ball. The team on **offense** tries to score a touchdown. The team on **defense** tries to stop them.

## Australia

A rugby ball is shaped like an American football but is rounder. In rugby, players can run and kick the ball forward but can pass it backward only.

## Ireland

In a **Gaelic** football game, players score by kicking or punching the ball into the other team's goal. The football is round, like a soccer ball.

Footgolf is gaining popularity around the world. It is a combination of soccer and golf.

## Mexico

Association football (also called soccer) is the most popular sport in Mexico. Players try to kick or head a ball past a goalkeeper.

## Thailand

In sepak takraw (SAY-pac TRAW-kaw), players pass the ball over a net without using their hands or arms. The small ball is made of **rattan**.

## Czech Republic

People here play a game called football tennis, or futnet. In futnet, players kick a soccer ball back and forth over a tennis net.

# GLOSSARY

**culture** (KUHL-chur) the ideas, customs, traditions, and way of life of a group of people

**defense** (DEE-fens) in sports, the side that tries to prevent the other team from scoring

**Gaelic** (GAY-lick) related to the Celtic people of Ireland or Scotland

**homemade** (HOME-MAYD) made by hand

**mirror** (MIR-ur) to clearly show exactly what another thing is like

**offense** (AW-fens) in sports, the team or part of a team that is attacking or trying to score

**rattan** (RAH-tan) a plant with long, strong stems that are woven together to make furniture, baskets, and other objects

**rhyme** (RIME) a short poem where each line ends with words that have the same ending sound

# INDEX

Afghanistan  4, 14, 15
Australia  18, 19, 28
Bolivia  20, 21
China  10
Czech Republic  29
Dominican Republic  4
France  16
Greece  4
Guatemala  26
India  27
Indonesia  22, 23
Ireland  27, 28
Malawi  5
Mexico  29
Nigeria  27
Philippines  8, 9
Thailand  29
Turkey  6, 7
United States  5, 6, 12, 16, 20, 26, 28
Zimbabwe  24, 25

## ABOUT THE AUTHOR

Growing up, John Perritano and his friends played "tennis ball" in the driveway. It was a cross between baseball and Wiffle ball but was played with a tennis ball.